MAKE IT OUT ALIVE IN A RAIN FOREST

Claudia Martin

PowerKiDS press.
New York

Published in 2018 by The Rosen Publishing Group
29 East 21st Street, New York, NY 10010

Produced for Rosen by Calcium
Editors: Sarah Eason and Jennifer Sanderson
Designer: Emma DeBanks
Picture Research: Rachel Blount
Illustrator: Venetia Dean

Picture credits: Cover: Shutterstock: Banana Republic images (bg), Jeep2499 (br). Inside:
Shutterstock: Allibum 25, Subbotina Anna 14, Mawardi Bahar 11, Gualberto Becerra 29, Ryan M.
Bolton 19, 27, Cienpies Design 42, Andre Dib 36, Filipe Frazao 44, Frontpage 8, 9, Fruzsi-Gergo
41t, Gavran333 5cr, Ramona Heim 39, Thanakorn Hongphan 47, Ammit Jack 38, JCLobo 15,
Kaulfuss Media 7, Fabio Lamanna 4, Lost Mountain Studio 30, Elena Mirage 35, Kotomiti Okuma
5tr, Pavel L Photo and Video 22, Ben Queenborough 13, Dr Morley Read 26, Montree Sanyos
20, Marco Schmidt 18, Elzbieta Sekowska 10, Sheykhan 5b, Aleksey Stemmer 40-41, Szefei 12,
Willem Tims 24, Toeytoey 33, Sergey Uryadnikov 28, VanHart 6, Santhosh Varghese 21, Vigen M
43, VladSer 34, Suwanon Wongsaphan 16; Wikimedia Commons: Jim Gathany/CDC 32, Marco
Schmidt 18.

Cataloging-in-Publication Data
Names: Martin, Claudia.
Title: Make it out alive in a rain forest / Claudia Martin.
Description: New York : PowerKids Press, 2018. | Series: Makerspace survival | Includes index.
Identifiers: ISBN 9781499434743 (pbk.) | ISBN 9781499434682 (library bound) | ISBN
9781499434569 (6 pack)
Subjects: LCSH: Jungle survival--Juvenile literature.
Classification: LCC GV200.5 M35 2018 | DDC 613.6'909152--dc23

Manufactured in China.

CPSIA Compliance Information: Batch BS17PK: For Further Information contact Rosen Publishing, New York, New York at 1-800-237-9932

Please note that the publisher **does not**
suggest readers carry out any practical
application of the Can You Make It?
activities and any other survival
activities in this book.

A note about measurements:
Measurements are given in U.S. form
with metric in parentheses. The metric
conversion is rounded to make it easier
to measure.

CONTENTS

Chapter 1

Survive the Rain Forest 4
World of Rain Forests 6
Rain Forest Peoples 8
Rain Forest Survivor 10

Chapter 2

Find Water 12
Plant Providers 14
Filtering Out 16

Chapter 3

Fill Your Stomach 18
Weaving Together 20
All Fired Up 22
Racking and Wrapping 24

Chapter 4

Time for Bed 26
Shelter Design 28
Get off the Ground 30

Chapter 5

Escape from Predators 32
Ravenous Rivers 34
Jungle Jaguars 36

Chapter 6

Make Your Way 38
Stick to It 40
Foot Care 42
Follow the Tracks 44

Answers—Did You Make It? 45
Glossary 46
Further Reading 47
Index 48

CHAPTER 1

SURVIVE
THE RAIN FOREST

You are about to be parachuted into the heart of a **tropical** rain forest. Completely alone, you must find your way back to civilization. To make your mission even harder, you cannot take with you any water, food, a tent, fire starters, or cooking equipment. How will you survive?

Will You Make It Out Alive?

You can dress in your choice of clothing and footwear. You can carry a **machete**. Apart from these essentials, you must provide yourself with food, water, and shelter by making your own tools and equipment. You are allowed to use any local materials you find in the rain forest, as well as any recyclable man-made items you can pick up. You will also be provided with a backpack in which you will find some interesting materials and tools.

What clothing and footwear would be suitable for your rain forest challenge?

What Is in Your Backpack?

The following materials and tools are in your backpack. When you come across a "Can You Make It?" activity in this book, you must choose from this list of items to construct it. Each item can be used only once. Study the list carefully before you set off. You can find the correct solutions for all the activities on page 45.

Can You Make It?

Materials
- 2 strong ropes, 4 feet (1 m) long
- Canvas, 7 feet x 4 feet (2 m x 1 m)
- Cord, 3 feet (1 m) long
- Crushed charcoal
- Elastic tubing
- Leather strip, 4 inches x 2 inches (10 cm x 5 cm)
- Plastic funnel
- Silk cloth

Rope

Tools
- Pocketknife
- Pair of scissors

Pocketknife

Pair of Scissors

Survival Tip
Use the Internet to look up all the items in your backpack before you begin your journey. Make sure you understand what they are and how you might be able to use them.

WORLD
OF RAIN FORESTS

You have probably never been to a tropical rain forest before, so take a few minutes to understand the **environment** you will be facing and its dangers.

Steamy Forests

Tropical rain forests are found near the equator, where it is usually hot and rainy. On average, more than 66 inches (168 cm) of rain falls there in a year. The average temperature is more than 75° F (24° C). In this climate, tall trees, known as broadleafs, dominate the land. Broadleafs have flat leaves and bear fruits. Since there is no cold season, the trees do not drop their leaves in the fall. They are **evergreen**. This is a rich environment for animal life: More than half the world's **species** are found in rain forests.

Key
1 Amazon Rain Forest
2 Congo River Basin Rain Forest
3 Southeast Asian Rain Forest

The largest tropical rain forests are in Central and South America, Central Africa, and Southeast Asia.

Layers of Forest

The rain forest has four layers. The highest layer has the tallest trees, called the **emergents**. These giant trees may reach 230 feet (70 m). This is where eagles, parrots, and bats hunt for insects, fruit, or small **mammals**. Below this layer is the **canopy**, where the trees form a roof of leaves over the forest beneath. Next is the shaded **understory**. Here you will find dangling vines and ferns clinging to the tree trunks. Howler monkeys and tree frogs jump from branch to branch in the understory. Few plants grow on the gloomy forest floor, unless a tree has fallen, allowing sunlight to reach the ground. Among the rotting fallen leaves, beetles, spiders, mice, and lizards roam. Snakes and jaguars lie waiting. Rivers weave their way between muddy banks.

Howler monkeys live in Central and South American rain forests. They are named for their loud calls.

RAIN FOREST
PEOPLES

You will find few **settlements** in the rain forest, but some peoples, such as the Kamayurá tribe of the Amazon, make it their home. They use the many plant and animal resources of the rain forest to survive. Before you set off on your challenge, pick up some maker skills from the Kamayurá.

Kamayurá Homes

Kamayurá homes are built of bent and interlocking branches, covered with sape grass. The Kamayurá know how to recognize *Daphnopsis* trees, from which a strong bark **fiber**, known as embira, can be pulled and used to make rope.

A key skill for the Kamayurá is weaving. Both boys and girls are taught to weave before marriage. Boys learn how to weave baskets from fibers such as buriti, taken from the moriche palm. Girls are taught to weave mats from grasses and hammocks from cotton. Hammocks are ideal for the rain forest because they keep the sleeper above the reach of crawling insects and snakes.

Kamayurá homes and meeting houses are covered with sape grass.

Finding Food

A large part of the Kamayurá diet is fish. Fish are caught in the Kuluene and Kuliseu Rivers, which flow into the Amazon River. One fishing method is to dam part of the river using rocks and sticks, then kill the trapped fish with poison made from the bark of the timbó vine. Nets tied from embira, and wooden bows and arrows, are also used.

A village is always surrounded by gardens cleared from the rain forest. Crops such as **cassava**, bananas, corn, and cotton are planted. Men go hunting for forest birds using their bows and arrows. Women go into the forest with their homemade baskets to pick wild berries and fruits, including *pequi* and *jenipapo*. They also collect wild honey, ants, turtle eggs, and firewood.

A man from the Kamayurá tribe is fishing in a canoe carved from the bark of the jatobá (courbaril) tree.

RAIN FOREST SURVIVOR

In 2011, a salesman named Minor Vidal was on a flight from Santa Cruz to Trinidad, in Bolivia. When the plane crashed into the Amazon Rain Forest, Minor began the fight of his life.

Collecting Resources

Minor crawled out of the wreckage with broken ribs and blood dripping from his head and arm. He was lucky—the other eight passengers and crew had died. Minor was a skilled camper and fisherman, so he had some survival and maker skills. He searched among the wreckage for items he could use. He found a lighter, a plastic bottle, and several watches. He strapped the watches to his arm to stop the bleeding. Looking around the site, he saw that there was no source of drinking water. He decided to leave, and using his own blood, he drew an arrow pointing in the direction he took.

Minor decided his best chance of survival was to stay by a river.

Plan of Action

Minor made his way to the bank of a nearby river, where he might be spotted from the air or the river itself. Knowing that dirt, **parasites**, and **bacteria** polluted the water, Minor constructed a water **filter** using several layers of his clothing and the plastic bottle. He set about catching fish and insects, using traps made from his hands and from sticks and stones.

When rescuers arrived at the wreckage, they realized one person was missing. They searched in the direction of the bloody arrow. Three days after the crash, a navy patrol boat caught sight of a man on the riverbank. Minor had made a flag to wave using his most brightly colored item of clothing and a stick. After being treated in the hospital, Minor went home to his wife and daughters.

In a survival situation, how could you use a plastic bottle?

FIERCE FACT!
In 1971, 17-year-old Juliane Koepcke survived nine days alone in the Amazon after a plane crash. Loggers found her.

CHAPTER 2

FIND WATER

You find yourself alone on the shady forest floor, many miles from a village or road. It is hot, and you are soon thirsty. You must meet your first basic survival need: safe drinking water.

Not a Drop to Drink

You would be right in thinking that there is plenty of water in the rain forest, but your problem is to find, or make, water that is safe to drink. Sometimes, you can see right away that decaying plants, animal dung, or mud has polluted water. Remember, though, that every inch of the rain forest teems with life, and the same can be said of the water that is found there. Even though you cannot see it, any water here may be carrying bacteria, which could cause illnesses such as **dysentery**, and parasites, which could take up residence inside your body.

This river could be a good source of water, but think about how you can safely drink from it.

Animal Signs

Forest animals also need water to drink, so look around for animal tracks or dung. If you see a lot of tracks all heading in one direction, they are likely to lead to water. Clouds of insects may mark the site of a water source. Flies stay within 300 feet (90 m) of water, so if one is buzzing around, water cannot be too far away.

The best source of water is a fast-flowing stream, but do not drink from the shallows. Here, insects and animal waste are likely to pollute the water. Even very shallow flowing water can knock you off your feet, so rig up a safety line using one of the items from your backpack before wading in. A safer choice would be to throw in a container attached to string, then haul it back toward yourself.

A South American tapir is drinking from a rain forest stream. The tapir is a plant eater, and the largest land mammal in the Amazon.

PLANT PROVIDERS

Look around: There are leaves and stems as far as you can see. All green plants need water to survive. They collect it through their roots or, sometimes, their leaves. Plants could be a good source of clean drinking water for you.

Use Your Machete

The water in a plant's stem is fairly safe to drink, unless the plant is poisonous. Look for the thicker, woody vines that twist around the trees, called **lianas**. Choose one that is around 2 inches (5 cm) thick and is not releasing a white, colored, or foul-smelling sap. Using your machete carefully, cut a piece about 5 feet (1.5 m) long, keeping both ends upward so the water does not dribble out. Fill a container with the water before drinking, so that insects do not tip into your mouth. Hold the water in your mouth before swallowing. Does it taste bitter? Is your mouth burning? If not, you can swallow it.

To make a container to hold your water, search for bamboo stems. These are stiff and hollow, apart from at the joints, where they are solid. When cutting a section, make sure that the bottom of it is just below a joint.

Bamboo stems are not hollow at the joints, which can be located by a horizontal mark on the outside of the plant.

Leaf Cup

Water that has fallen directly from the sky onto a plant or into a clean container should be free of parasites and bacteria. Large leaves are good at collecting rainwater and dew. A simple water collection technique is to angle a large leaf toward a container placed on the ground. Overnight, the steady dripping from the leaf should give you a mouthful or two of water in the morning.

FIERCE FACT!
To test if it is safe to drink water, collect some in a container. Sprinkle fine sand on top of the water. If the sand floats, the water is **dense** and therefore polluted.

Bromeliads are a type of plant that live on the branches of rain forest trees. They collect water between their leaves. Boil it before drinking.

FILTERING OUT

A filter is a device with small holes in it, large enough for water to pass through, but too small for solid **particles**. Dripping muddy water through a filter will remove dirt and larger parasites. After filtering water, always finish by boiling it to kill any tiny bacteria.

Water Filter

A filter can be made by passing water through smaller and smaller holes, until few impurities remain. Natural materials can be used as filters, such as stones, gravel, and sand. Stones will prevent large particles from passing through. Sand will block much smaller particles. Woven cloth contains small holes; the finer the cloth, the smaller the holes.

Charcoal is a black solid made from burned **organic** materials, such as wood. When many substances pass through charcoal, they stick to its surface and are trapped. For this reason, charcoal is used in household water filters.

FIERCE FACT!
At home, you can experiment with filtering water by adding impurities, such as pieces of paper and cooking oil. Do not drink the filtered water!

This water is obviously polluted with mud, but it may also contain parasites and bacteria.

Make a Water Filter

From your list of supplies and local materials, you will need to make:

→ A container for your filter, into which dirty water can be poured
→ Several layers of materials that will filter out smaller and smaller impurities
→ A cup or other container to collect filtered water.

Can You Make It?

Step 1

Think about which item you will use to create the container for your filter. You will need to pour water into this.

Step 2

Which two items from your backpack could be used as filters? Consider how they can be held inside your container.

Step 3

What local materials could be collected and used to create extra filtering layers?

Step 4

Which local materials could be used to collect water that has traveled through your filter? Turn back to pages 14–15 for a hint.

Filter

Filtering layers

Container

Filtered water container

Water

CHAPTER 3
FILL YOUR STOMACH

The effort of finding water has made you hungry. There is plenty of food in the rain forest, but you must be careful searching for it because many plants and insects here are poisonous. To avoid a deadly mistake, you need the help of a Kamayurá tribesperson or other knowledgeable adult.

Fruits of the Forest

When hunting for **edible** plants, if you do not recognize it, do not eat it. In fact, do not even touch the plant. Some rain forest plants have developed fierce methods of protecting themselves from being eaten. For example, if you are in the tropical forests of northern Australia, do not brush against stinging trees. Their leaves are covered in hairs that cause a painful reaction in human skin.

Edible fruits in the rain forest include banana, mango, fig, and papaya. Look for coconuts, which you can open with a careful blow from your machete. **Starchy** roots will give you energy. Depending on the region, these may include taro and yam. Both of these plants grow wild in tropical regions and have also been planted as crops for thousands of years. Once identified, roots can be dug up using your machete, then boiled.

Yam plants store food in swollen underground stems. Try boiling, frying, or roasting them.

Entomophagy

The eating of insects, called entomophagy, is widely practiced by rain forest peoples. However, never try to catch a hairy, spiny, stinging, or biting insect. Do not touch insects that are brightly colored, since this may be a warning to **predators** that they are poisonous. Not all ants are edible, but if you can spot the giant leaf-cutting ants, known as *hormiga culona* ("big-bottomed ant" in Spanish), they will make quite a tasty meal. The roasted queen ants are a delicacy in Colombia.

FIERCE FACT!
Although insect-eating is rare in the United States, around 2 billion people around the world regularly eat around 1,900 edible insect species.

"Big bottomed ants" could make a tasty snack.

WEAVING TOGETHER

The Kamayurá are experts at using plant fibers to knot nets for catching fish and to weave baskets for collecting berries. To do the same, you will need to recognize suitable plants and learn a basic weaving technique.

Palm Fibers

Palm trees are a good source of fibers. Fibers taken from their leaves are strong and stiff, making them good for baskets, hats, and mats. The Kamayurá strip fibers from the leaves of the moriche palm to weave baskets. Raffia, which you may use for crafts at home, is the torn and dried leaves of the raffia palm.

Bast fibers, which are stripped from the inner bark of a tree, are strong but usually more flexible than leaf fibers. Sugar palms are a common source of bast fibers in tropical regions. Coir is a fiber taken from the hairy outer husk of a coconut. Once twisted and knotted, it makes an ideal fishing net. When you find a palm tree, experiment with its fibers to see what products it would suit.

Coir, from the husk of a coconut, is strong and fairly waterproof.

Weaving Technique

To weave a basic circular basket, collect straight "spokes" of tough fiber to form the frame. Lay them in a clocklike pattern, crossing at the center. You must now weave softer fibers, called "weavers," in and out of the spokes in an under-over pattern. If the previous weaver has passed under a spoke, make sure the next weaver passes over it. Twist the ends of your weavers into the pattern, so that they do not come loose. Curl your spokes into a bowl shape as you go. When you have formed your basket, secure the ends of your spokes and weavers to finish off. Tuck the ends back through the weave, so they cannot escape.

Examine how this maker has passed the weavers over and under the raffia spokes.

FIERCE FACT!

The leaves of the *Raphia regalis* raffia palm are the longest of any plant, reaching 82 feet (25 m). Each leaf is made of around 180 leaflets.

ALL FIRED UP

To cook food and boil filtered water, you must light a fire. With no matches, you need to use your maker skills to get a spark. Remember: Fire is always dangerous. Never start a fire without an adult's help.

Bow Drill

A bow drill rubs together two pieces of wood. This creates **friction**, making a burning **ember** among the flakes of rubbed-off wood. This ember is then tipped onto a pile of dry bark flakes or straw to set it on fire.

A bow drill is made of four parts: fireboard, spindle, bow, and block. The fireboard and spindle must be made of dry, dead wood. The fireboard is carved with a circular dent. The spindle is spun around and around in the dent, until an ember is made. The bow is used to turn the spindle. The block is a piece of wood or stone with a notch in it. It is pressed down on the spindle to hold it in place.

This boy is spinning his spindle with his bare hands.

Make a Bow Drill

From your list of supplies, you will need to make:

→ A fireboard carved with a circular dent and a notch, through which embers fall onto a strip of bark for collection
→ A spindle that fits into the circular dent and can be spun around
→ A bow to spin the spindle
→ A block to press down on the spindle.

Can You Make It?

Step 1

Think about which local material to use for your fireboard and spindle. Which tool could you use to carve your fireboard and taper the ends of your spindle?

Step 2

Which item from your backpack could be used as the cord for your bow? What local material will form the rest of your bow?

Step 3

Which local material could be used as your block? Hint: You will need material you can carve a notch into.

Step 4

Wrap the bow cord several times around your spindle. With one hand, press down on the top of the spindle with the block. With your other hand, spin the spindle by moving the bow horizontally.

Block

Spindle

Bow

Fireboard

RACKING
AND WRAPPING

You do not have a cooking pot, so use your maker skills to boil water and heat your food. At home, we often use pots made of metal and pottery, which do not burn or melt at the temperatures that cook food. Think about how the materials you choose will react to heat.

Plank Cooking

Wood will burn if you put it directly into flames, so if you use wood for your cooking utensils, keep it a little distance from the fire, and watch it closely. A roll of bark or a hollowed-out plank or stem could hold food near to the fire. Experiment to see how hot the food or water becomes at this distance, since it may take a long time to heat up.

An alternative is to pin a piece of fish or meat to a plank using nails made of sharpened chunks of wood. Tilt the plank toward the flames, but keep it just out of their reach.

You could roast a fresh fish using wooden utensils.

Build a Rack

To slow roast vegetables or a piece of meat or fish, build a rack to hold it. Hunt for flexible, but strong, vines or branches. Bend one into a loop, then tie the loop closed with palm fiber or strong grasses. Tie a couple of crossbars of vine across the loop. You have created a tennis racket shape! Finally, tie a flexible branch down the length of the rack. The vegetables can be wedged between this branch and the crossbars. Now balance your rack on a pile of stones, so that it is just beyond the lick of the flames.

Wrap food in banana leaves, then place it directly into hot ashes. The leaves are not poisonous, but they are hard to digest, so unwrap the food before eating it.

FIERCE FACT!
The oldest cooking pots found by archaeologists are made of baked clay and are around 20,000 years old. They were found in a cave in China.

CHAPTER 4
TIME FOR BED

The sun is dipping. Soon, it will be too dim beneath the rain forest canopy to see your hand in front of your face. You must find a safe spot to camp before it is too late.

Pick a Spot

When choosing a spot to camp for the night, look for higher ground, where the soil will be drier. Do not camp near swamps or rivers, as mosquitoes, which live close to water, will surround them. Water sources also attract large animals, including predators such as big cats like jaguars. If there is heavy rain during the night, rivers could flood their banks, and dry riverbeds could turn into raging waters. Do not lie down under a tall tree either—it is likely to be an old tree, which could drop a branch if the wind picks up. The same goes for trees with heavy nuts or fruit.

The flooded rain forest is home to many species of fish, including piranhas.

Dig a Ditch

Clear your camping area of fallen leaves, rocks, and logs. These could all be hiding places for snakes, spiders, and insects. Use a stick rather than your hands to sweep them away. Now, using a tough stick, dig a ditch around your camp. This will allow water to drain away if it rains, which it is likely to, given that you are in the rain forest.

Light a series of small fires around the edges of your camp. Flames and smoke will keep away insects and predators. Adding damp leaves to the flames will create more smoke. If you can recognize lemongrass, these leaves are said to be a particularly effective mosquito **repellent** if burned.

Examine your camping area for hazards. Tree-dwelling tarantulas, such as the Malaysian earth tiger, may be hiding in hollow trunks.

SHELTER DESIGN

The main purpose of a rain forest shelter is to keep rain off your head as you sleep. You can construct a basic shelter using only your machete and the materials you find around you in the forest.

Roof Overhead

To put a roof over your head, make a pole by hacking off a straight, slim branch, perhaps 6 feet (2 m) long. Wedge your pole horizontally between two trees, pressing it between their branches. Make sure the pole is about 4 feet (1 m) off the ground. Lianas, the vines you can see dangling from the trees around you, are the natural rope of the rain forest. Cut a few fairly thin lianas, which can be easily coiled and tied. Knot your pole in place.

Cut two more slim branches, about 6 to 7 feet (1.8–2 m) long. Lean these two poles at either end of your first roof pole, creating a sideways V shape with the ground. You will sleep inside this V. Secure these poles with liana. Add one or two light poles between the two slanting poles to give strength to your structure.

Some rain forest shelters are built on stilts to protect them from rising river waters.

Thatching

Palm leaves are ideal to thatch, or cover, your roof, since they are large and waterproof. Many species of palms are used for thatching around the world, including fan palms. Watch out for snakes, tarantulas, and other biters as you collect your leaves. Thread dozens of palm leaves onto a liana, like beads on a necklace. Tie the liana between your slanting poles. You will need to thread a second or even a third liana with leaves to cover the entire roof.

Tree-dwelling snakes, such as pit vipers, have been known to hide in palm leaves while they wait for prey.

FIERCE FACT!

The Korowai tribe of the Indonesian rain forest build tree houses on stilts up to 140 feet (43 m) high to protect them from flooding and attack.

GET OFF THE GROUND

You will sleep more easily if you are not on the ground. On a raised bed constructed from branches or swinging in a hammock, you will be out of the reach of snakes and crawling insects.

Hang a Hammock

The Kamayurá sleep in hammocks, which they weave from cotton. You could also make a hammock by knotting together strong fibers, using a similar method to making a traditional fishing net. A simpler method of constructing a hammock is to use a prewoven piece of strong fabric and one or two pieces of rope. The shorter sides of the fabric are gathered together and tied with a large knot. Your hammock must be suspended between two trees, from the rafters of a house, or from a specially made wood or metal frame.

When working with rope, it is handy to know at least one basic knot. A useful knot to master is the lark's head, also known as the cow hitch. It is used for tying rope to another object. To make it, wrap a loop of rope around the object to be attached. Pass the ends of the rope through the loop. Pull tight. Bear in mind that a hammock is only as strong as the knots you tie.

This hammock has been constructed from knotted cotton fibers and wooden strips.

Make a Hammock

From your list of supplies and local materials, you will need to make:

→ A hammock that is large enough to sleep in and strong enough to take your weight

→ A means of tying the hammock between two trees.

Can You Make It?

Step 1
Think about which item from your backpack could be used as fabric for your hammock.

Step 2
Which items from your backpack could be used to tie your hammock to two trees?

Step 3
Consider the shape of a hammock. How will you gather your hammock at each end?

Step 4
Which knots could tie the hammock fabric to the rope? You will need to use different knots to tie the rope ends to the trees.

Rope

Hammock

Knots to tie rope to trees

Knot to tie hammock fabric to rope

CHAPTER 5
ESCAPE
FROM PREDATORS

Top predators, or apex predators, are animals that prey on other creatures but are usually too fierce to be turned into meals themselves. In the rain forest, top predators are the big cats and powerful reptiles, such as snakes and crocodiles. Running away from a top predator will do no good. You will need to use your maker skills to survive.

Malaria Mosquitoes

The deadliest animal in the rain forest is one of the smallest. Every year, mosquitoes kill around 725,000 people, more than any other animal. Mosquitoes carry diseases, such as **malaria**, from person to person. A mosquito's bite can pass malaria parasites from the mosquito's saliva into your blood. The parasites travel to your liver, where they cause fever, vomiting, and, if untreated, death.

Malaria is spread by female Anopheles *mosquitoes, which live in tropical regions.*

This human blood, seen under a microscope, is infected with malaria parasites.

Makers to the Rescue

Malaria is common in tropical regions, including rain forests. Many of the world's poorest people live in these areas, and they cannot afford mosquito repellent or the medicine that kills malaria parasites. Makers decided to solve the problem. Most mosquito bites happen when the victim is sleeping. Makers developed inexpensive mosquito nets made from hard-wearing man-made fabrics, such as polyester. They experimented with how to cover nets in mosquito-killing **insecticide** that does not easily wash off. Today, the nets they invented are given out for free in malaria-infected areas.

Since you do not have a mosquito net, you must construct your own protection. Cut up a spare T-shirt, so that it can be tied around your forehead, with a fringe of vertical strips to cover your face and neck. At night, run liana vines between two trees, and use clothing and large leaves to create a net over your sleeping area.

RAVENOUS RIVERS

There are many reasons to stay out of the water in the rain forest, from sharp-toothed piranhas to shocking electric eels. However, if a river is barring your way, what can you do? Build your way across it!

Beware Water

If you find yourself on the banks of the Amazon River or one of its **tributaries**, keep an eye out for black caimans. These are close relatives of crocodiles and alligators. Caimans can grow to 16 feet (5 m) long and are known to snatch animals as large as horses when they come to the river to drink. During the **dry season**, when water levels fall, do not swim in isolated pools. Red-bellied piranhas may collect here in large numbers. Although humans are not their usual prey, they could inflict nasty bites. Among the other dangerous fish in the Amazon are electric eels, which can generate an electric current inside their body. It is forceful enough to knock you over in the water.

The black caiman is the largest predator in the Amazon River.

Get Across

To cross water, one option is to build a raft. As you have discovered, bamboo stems are hollow, which makes them very **buoyant**. Using a liana, lash together a few stems of bamboo, with a couple of running crosswise for added strength.

How wide is the river you want to cross? Bamboo stems grow to 65 feet (20 m) tall. Bamboo is often used for construction in tropical regions, since it is strong and usually bends under pressure rather than snaps. The strongest stems will be thicker and shorter. How could you use bamboo poles and lianas to construct a bridge across a stream or swamp?

This simple bridge across a narrow stream is made of bamboo stems.

JUNGLE JAGUARS

The fiercest predators in any rain forest are the big cats. In Central and South America, jungle cats include jaguars and cougars. In Africa, you might meet leopards, and in Asia, watch out for tigers.

Slingshot

Jaguars grow to 6 feet (2 m) long and have sharp teeth for crunching and ripping through bones and flesh. They feed only on meat, from birds to monkeys. Alone in the rain forest, you will be at risk from jaguars if you step into their territory. Protect yourself by making a slingshot to startle them into running away.

A slingshot has a Y-shaped frame, to which an elastic string is tied. A pouch attached to the string holds a **projectile**. When you stretch back the string, you store **elastic potential energy** in it. This is "possible" energy, or energy that could make something happen. When the string is released, the potential energy turns into movement. The projectile flies through the air.

The jaguar is the world's third-largest cat, after the tiger and lion.

Make a Slingshot

From your list of supplies and local materials, you will need to make:

→ A strong Y-shaped frame
→ An elastic string that can be securely attached to the frame
→ A pouch to hold a projectile.

Can You Make It?

Step 1
Think about which local item you will use as your Y-shaped frame. You may find it useful to carve notches in your frame where the elastic string will be attached.

Step 2
Which item in your backpack could be used as elastic string?

Step 3
Consider which item in your backpack could form the pouch. You will need to make holes in it to thread through and then tie the elastic string to the pouch.

Step 4
Experiment with your slingshot using a soft projectile. What happens if you adjust the length of the elastic string?

Elastic string

Notches

Pouch

Y-shaped frame

FIERCE FACT!
To practice with your slingshot, fire soft paper balls. Never fire at a person or animal, as you will injure them.

CHAPTER 6
MAKE YOUR WAY

The time has come to find a village and make your way out of the forest. You do not have a map or a compass to guide you, but this region is just a featureless green patch on the map anyway! How will you get home?

Try to Walk

Walking through the rain forest is harder than you might think. Where the canopy is thick, it is dim on the forest floor. With less sunlight to make food, few plants tangle about your feet, and you find it fairly easy to make progress. However, where trees have fallen, sunlight and high rainfall have grown a dense thicket of shrubs, ferns, and lianas.

To get anywhere at all, you must hack at the vegetation with your machete. You will find it easier to cut stems and branches at an angle. Cut downward to sever tough stalks and lianas. Cut upward to slash leaves. Always cut away from your body with a flick of the wrist. This is exhausting work, and sometimes you can progress only 0.5 miles (0.8 km) in a whole day.

This Huaoroni hunter is using a blowgun and darts tipped with plant poison. The Huaoroni live in the western Amazon.

Navigate

To your untrained eyes, the rain forest seems the same everywhere you look. Children of rain forest tribes soon learn to recognize the different plants and pathways in the territory surrounding their village. When hunting, tribesmen usually travel in a group, communicating with each other through calls and whistles. To get a bird's eye view of their surroundings, they may tie their feet together with lianas and shin up trees. So that you do not walk in circles, leave markers to show yourself where you have been. These markers should not be edible, and they should be brightly colored.

FIERCE FACT!
Many rain forest hunters use sharp darts with poisoned tips. They blow the darts out of a hollow stem or branch.

Have you passed this way before? Tie a marker to a tree, so you will recognize it next time.

STICK TO IT

Bacteria and fungi thrive in the hot, damp conditions in the rain forest. Be careful that you do not receive a bite or scratch, as it could quickly become infected with these organisms. To avoid such injuries, use a stick to beat the undergrowth as you walk.

Look Down

As you walk, look down at your feet. You are watching for animals that could bite or sting you and any plants with sharp thorns. By using your stick to sweep to left and right ahead of you, you are announcing your arrival to snakes and spiders. If they are able, they will move out of your way, but watch out for shed skins or snakes. Snakes shed their worn and parasite-covered skins a few times a year. This makes them sluggish, so they can more easily be stepped on, which could result in a bite.

Snakebite!

If a snake bites you, call for help. Keep the bitten area below your heart to reduce the spread of **venom** around your body through your bloodstream. If you were bitten on an arm or leg, make a splint with a stick, loosely tied with grass to keep the limb still and slow the venom.

Watch out for snakes, such as this Madagascan giant hognose, hiding in the undergrowth.

Quicksand

Use your stick to test the strength of the ground so you do not step into a swamp or quicksand. Quicksand is a mixture of sand, mud, and water, and may be found around the edges of rivers and lakes. If you do step in quicksand, throw off your backpack to lighten yourself, so that you do not sink in. Lie on your back to spread your weight. Wriggle and swim your way free before the quicksand hardens and you are trapped.

Do not step into a swamp. You have no idea how deep the water is or what is beneath the surface.

FIERCE FACT!
The Brazilian wandering spider has the most powerful venom of any spider. It hides in the leaves of banana plants and bromeliads.

FOOT CARE

Keeping your feet and legs healthy is the only way you will get out of the rain forest, so use your creativity to protect them from infection and bloodsucking beasts. Think of ways to make new shoes, or construct leg protectors known as puttees.

Puttee Protection

If you leave any skin exposed, you are at risk from creatures that latch onto other animals to feed on their blood. These include ticks and some species of leech. If you see one on your skin, do not just pull it. Pulling it will leave a nasty wound that could become infected. To remove a tick, tie a cotton thread around the tick's mouthparts, then pull without twisting. For a leech, pull your skin taut, then slide a fingernail under the sucker.

To prevent bloodsuckers from finding your skin, tuck your pants into your boots. Roll down your sleeves, and turn up your collar. Construct puttees to stop thorns from ripping your pants. To do this, cut large strips of bark, and wrap them around your legs using lianas or grasses.

This adventurer is wearing store-bought puttees, but you will have to improvise with local materials.

Keeping Dry

Wearing wet or sweaty clothing could lead to a skin infection, as bacteria will multiply in the damp warmth. If you have a change of clothes, dry wet ones on a stick as you walk. Your feet are particularly at risk of infection. Sneakers will quickly become waterlogged if you walk through a swamp or wet undergrowth, which could cause the skin to blister and swell. If you had plastic bags, you could tie them over your shoes to keep them dry. If your shoes start to rot, you could construct new ones using waterproof leaves, tough bark, and grasses.

FIERCE FACT!
The giant Amazonian leech can grow to 17 inches (43 cm) long. It feeds on the blood of other animals.

These shoes have been woven from bark fiber. Which fibers could you use?

FOLLOW THE TRACKS

Most villages are close to a water source, so your best chance of rescue is to follow a river. If you head downhill in the rain forest and follow animal tracks going the same way, you are likely to reach water.

Bamboo Blower

There is one last use that you can find for bamboo before you leave the forest. The hollow stems can be turned into a wind instrument or whistle to attract attention. Cut a slim stem and carve a hole, so that you can blow into the side like a flute. Experiment with how you can change the sound by adding extra holes or sliding a smaller stem inside.

You Survived!

You notice a series of hoof tracks, all heading in one direction, and you follow them to the banks of a river. As you follow the water downstream, you notice a garden in a clearing. Cotton and cassava are growing. You blow your bamboo whistle, and a Kamayurá family appear. You gratefully accept their offer of a hammock for the night.

You are given a warm welcome in the village and a bowl of sweet cassava soup called mohete.

ANSWERS—
DID YOU MAKE IT?

Did your makerspace survival skills pass the test? Did you select the best equipment for each "Make It Out Alive" activity? Check your choices against the answers below.

Page 17 Water Filter

Crushed charcoal • Plastic funnel
Silk cloth
The plastic funnel could be a container for your filter. Crushed charcoal, inside the silk cloth, could be used as the filter. On top, you could layer sand, gravel, then stones. As shown on pages 14–15, a bamboo stem could collect the water.

Page 23 Bow Drill

Cord, 3 feet (1 m) long
Pocketknife
Collect dry, dead wood to use for your fireboard and spindle. Using your pocketknife, strip away the bark. Taper the base of your spindle to a flat point so it fits snugly in the fireboard. The spindle's other end should be sharper. The bow can be made of cord tied to a long branch. Carve a deep hole in hard wood for your block.

Page 31 Hammock

2 strong ropes, 4 feet (1 m) long
Canvas, 7 feet x 4 feet (2 m x 1 m)
Use the canvas for your hammock. Gather the shorter sides of the canvas, and tie a chunky knot at each end. Using the rope, make a lark's head knot around each end of the hammock below the knot in the canvas, which will stop the lark's head from slipping. Secure the ends of the rope by looping them around a tree several times, running the rope through the loops and tying multiple knots.

Page 37 Slingshot

Elastic tubing • Leather strip
Pair of scissors
A strong, dry forked stick could make your frame. The elastic tubing could be used as string. The leather strip will make a good pouch. Shortening the length of the elastic tubing will make your slingshot fire more forcefully.

GLOSSARY

bacteria Tiny living things that can cause disease.

buoyant Able to float.

canopy The upper branches of forest trees, forming an almost unbroken layer of leaves.

cassava The starchy root of a tropical tree.

dense Closely packed.

dry season In the tropics, a yearly period of low rainfall.

dysentery A severe infection causing diarrhea.

edible Safe to eat.

elastic potential energy Energy stored in stretched elastic.

ember Small piece of glowing wood from a fire.

emergents Trees taller than the surrounding trees.

environment The natural world, or surroundings, in a particular place.

evergreen Describes a plant that does not lose its leaves in winter.

fiber Thin thread of animal, plant, or man-made material.

filter A device with small holes in it to remove impurities, particularly from water.

friction The force that slows down an object when it is moving against another object or material.

fungi Living things, including mushrooms, that get their food from decaying organic material.

impurities Dirt or other unwanted substances.

insecticide A substance for killing insects.

lianas Woody, climbing plants.

logging Cutting down trees to use their wood.

machete A large, wide-bladed knife.

malaria A disease caused by a parasite that is spread by mosquitoes.

mammals Group of animals with body hair that feed their young with milk.

organic Coming from living things.

parasites Living things that live in or on another living thing.

particles Tiny pieces.

predators Animals that kill or eat other animals.

projectile An object that is thrown forward.

repellent A substance that keeps away insects or other pests.

settlements Villages, towns, or other communities of people.

species A group of similar living things that can breed with each other.

starchy Containing a lot of starch, an important source of energy.

tributaries Rivers or streams flowing into a larger river.

tropical In an area around the equator, where it is hot and often rainy.

understory The trees and shrubs growing between the canopy and the forest floor.

venom Poisonous substance injected into prey by biting or stinging.

FURTHER READING

Books

Clarke, Ginjer L. *What's Up in the Amazon Rain Forest*. New York, NY: Grosset & Dunlap, 2015.

Editors of *TIME for Kids Magazine. All About Survival* (TIME for Kids Book of How). New York, NY: TIME for Kids, 2014.

Graves, Colleen and Aaron. *The Big Book of Makerspace Projects*. New York, NY: McGraw-Hill Education, 2016.

Hardyman, Robyn. *Surviving the Rainforest* (Sole Survivor). New York, NY: Gareth Stevens, 2016.

Websites

Due to the changing nature of Internet links, PowerKids Press has developed an online list of websites related to the subject of this book. This site is updated regularly. Please use this link to access the list: www.powerkidslinks.com/ms/rainforest

INDEX

A
Amazon Rain Forest, 10, 35

B
bamboo, 14, 35, 44–45
big cats, 26, 32, 36

C
caimans, 34
canopy, 7, 26, 38
clothing, 4, 11, 33, 43
cooking, 4, 24–25

F
farming, 7
fire, 4, 22, 24, 27
food, 4, 9, 18, 22, 24, 38
forest floor, 7, 12, 38
fruits, 6–7, 9, 18, 26

H
hammocks, 8, 30–31, 44–45

I
insects, 7–8, 11, 13–14, 18–19, 27, 30

K
Kamayurá, 8–9, 18, 20, 44

L
lianas, 14, 28–29, 33, 35, 38–39, 42
logging, 7

M
mining, 7
mosquitoes, 26, 32–33

P
palms, 8, 20–21, 25, 29
plants, 7–8, 12, 14–15, 18, 20–21,
   38–39, 40–41
predators, 19, 26–27, 32, 36

Q
quicksand, 41

R
raft, 38
reptiles, 32
rivers, 7, 9, 11, 26–27, 34–35, 41, 44
roots, 14, 18

S
settlements, 8
shelter, 4, 28
snakes, 7–8, 27, 29–30, 32, 35, 40–41
spiders, 7, 27, 40–41

T
trees, 6–8, 14, 18, 20, 26, 28–31, 33,
   38–39, 45

U
understory, 7

V
Vidal, Minor, 10–11

W
water, 4, 10–18, 22, 24, 26–27, 34–35,
   41, 44–45
weaving, 8, 20–21